How To Tie A Bow

In all the years I have done wedding flowers, one thing really stands out as the skill that amazes most people, tying bows. This, in turn, always amazes me because I genuinely believe that everyone can learn to make bows. It takes just a bit of practice and some persistence. At times you may feel like you have ten thumbs, but remember, everyone felt that way, including myself.

There are only a few steps to making a bow. It is simply learning to loop, pinch and twist the ribbon. The secret is in securing the loops together. The wire (or strand of ribbon) must be pulled as tight as possible. Even if the loops are not perfect, they can be adjusted if the wire is tight enough to keep the bow from falling apart.

To really learn bows, allow a little practice time. Buy an inexpensive bolt of ribbon and make ten to twenty small bows. If you don't have a full bolt, allow 3 yards of ribbon for each practice bow. Remember, it is not the size that matters, but the method. I'm here to tell you, it only gets easier.

1 Pinch the ribbon 4" to 6" up from the end, between your thumb and first two fingers. Make sure the "good" side is face up.

2 Make a loop of any size moving the ribbon up over your hand and back around to be pinched between your fingers. The back side of the ribbon should be showing below your hand.

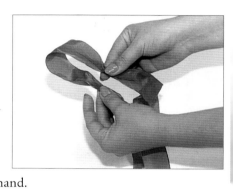

3 Here you need to twist the ribbon for the "good" side to be face up again. Make the twist close to your fingers and hold onto it.

4 After the twist, loop the ribbon around below your hand and catch it again between your fingers. Pinch it to keep it in place.

5a Continue twisting the ribbon, looping it around then pinching it at the end of the loop.

5b Make 4 or 5 loops on either side of your fingers.

6 After making the loops, cut the ribbon 4" to 6" past the loops. These loose ends are the bow "tails" or "streamers".

To finish, (this is the important part) you will need to wrap a wire or a separate piece of ribbon around the center to take the place of your fingers.

7a Wire: Bend a floral wire in half. Place the bent center of the wire under your thumb, over the center of the bow. With your other hand, twist the ends

of the wire together as tight as possible under the bow. If you need to, use pliers to tighten. Be careful not to break the wire.

7b Ribbon: This takes a little more practice. Cut an 18" strip of ribbon and tie a knot in the center. Place the knot under your thumb, over the center of the

bow. Wrap the ends of the ribbon around the back of the bow and knot them tightly together.

8 Fluff out the loops and adjust them until the bow looks right to you. This can be done by placing a finger in the middle of a loop and gently pulling outward and upward.

That is how every bow is made whether you have two loops or twenty. Just remember to loop, pinch then twist as you go.

You may be wondering why I used wire and ribbon to finish the bow. Wire can be inserted like a "stem" or used as a hanger. The ribbon can be used to tie the bow onto something. One will work better than the other depending on your project.

Using a bow wire

Tying on a bow

I f you have physical limitations to tying bows or are just so frustrated that you want to scream, try some of these alternatives. These methods are a little slower, but the success rate is inspiring.

The E•Z Bow Maker™ is a measuring base with upright dowels to pinch the ribbon while you make the loops. It is also numbered to show each loop size in inches. All you have to do is loop and twist. Your bow comes out perfect. Every loop is exact and the dowels don't get hand cramps while they pinch the ribbon.

1   Place a floral wire between the dowels so it is under the bow when you finish.

2   Place the ribbon between the dowels, 4" to 6" from the end to allow for a tail.

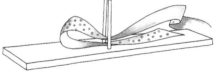

3   Twist the ribbon so the back side is up and loop it around, making the largest loop of the bow.

4   Continue making loops on either side. Graduate the sizes from large to small until you reach the center.

5   Make a small loop for the center, another tail, then cut the ribbon. Pull the wire from the bottom around the bow, through the center loop. Tighten the wire and wrap it around to the back.

The Basic Faux Bow can be made any size by cutting the strips of ribbon longer or shorter. By making bows this way, you eliminate all pinching and twisting.

1   Cut single lengths of ribbon to make loops. Cut one 3" strip for the center then two 4", two 5", two 7" and two 8" strips for the sides.

2   Fold each section in half and glue the ends together. Scrunch the ends as you glue them to give the bow a "tied" look.

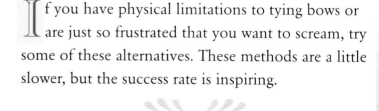

3   Lay the two largest sections end to end, and glue one over the other. Add the rest of the loops from large to small, gluing them to the center.

4   Glue the center loop in last to cover the ends. Cut two more strips of ribbon and glue them to the back as tails.

Purchase your E•Z Bow Maker at your local craft or fabric store or send $11.95 plus $3.50 shipping & handling to: Mark Publishing, 5400 Scotts Valley Dr., Scotts Valley, CA 95066 Phone: (408) 438-7668

Wired Loops are quick to make and help add a touch of ribbon to any arrangement. They can be placed close together to give the appearance of a bow or used to add texture and color between flowers.

1 Make a small loop of ribbon and wire it to a wooden pick for a single loop.

2 Use a little more ribbon to add on a single or double tail. After looping the ribbon, bend it back up and cut it. Add separate pieces for more tails and wire them to a wood pick.

3 Multiple loops can be made by just looping the ribbon around in the same direction . Tails can be added if desired.

The Tailored Bow is perfect for packages and hair barrettes. Once it is put together, simply tape or glue it in place.

1 Cut 3 different lengths of ribbon. Overlap the ends and staple the centers.

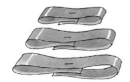

2 Stack the loops and staple them all together.

3 Wrap a length of ribbon around the center and glue the ends.

4 Optional: glue pointed tails to the back.

Once you have mastered the loop, pinch and twist technique, you are ready to refine your bows. There are many types of bows, these are just a few that are commonly used in weddings.

The Loopy Bow is made by keeping all the loops the same size, no matter what that size may be.

The Floral Bow can be made any size. What makes it a floral bow is graduating the sizes of the loops.

1 Pinch the ribbon and make a loop leaving the tail the desired length.

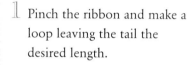

2 Continue making loops gradually increasing the size of the loops until the bow is full and you have enough ribbon left to make the other tail.

3 Secure the center of the bow with wire.

4 Fan out the loops.

5 Cut the tails at an angle or in points to finish off the bow.

1 Pinch the ribbon and make a loop leaving the tail the desired length.

2 Continue making loops keeping them uniform in size until the bow is full, then make the other tail.

3 Secure the center with floral wire.

4 Fan out the loops.

5 Cut the tails at an angle or in points to finish off the bow.

The Layered Bow is two (or more) separate bows stacked on top of each other. They can be glued in place or held together by the wires.

1 Make two (or more) separate bows, in various sizes and finish them with wire.

2 Lay the smaller bow over the center of the larger bow and connect the wires by twisting them together under the larger bow.

The Overlay Bow is made by stacking two (or more) ribbons of various sizes before you tie the bow. Lace ribbon over a solid color is a beautiful combination.

1 To keep the ribbons in place, add a dab of glue to the ends before you start to make the bow.

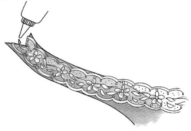

2 Make any size or style of bow you choose.

The Multiple-Ribbon Bow is made by combining several ribbons close to the same size, but in various colors or textures.

1 Pinch the ribbons together and loop them around as if they were just one. Pinch them again and twist them face up if needed.

2 Continue making the bow and finishing it just like you would for a single ribbon.

Ribbon Sizes & Ribbon Roses

Ribbon Sizes

The size of a ribbon is usually referred to by a number. The captions here show the number with the standard size it refers to.

#16
Approx. 2" or 56mm

#9
Approx.1 1/4" or 39mm

#5
Approx. 7/8" or 23mm

#40
Approx. 2 3/4" or 77mm

#3
Approx. 5/8" or 15mm

#1
Approx. 3/8" or 9mm

Ribbon Roses

Wired Roses

1 Cut a length of wired ribbon and tie one end in a knot.

2 Pull a wire from one side of the ribbon, gathering the ribbon as you pull.

3 Wrap the gathered side around the knot as tightly as possible to form the "petals". At the end, fold in the ribbon and wrap the remaining wire tightly around the base of the "petals".

Regular Ribbon

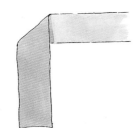

1   Fold ribbon at a right angle, leaving 2" for a tail.

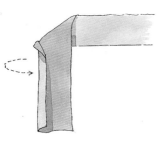

2   Roll the outside edge tightly to the inside a few times to make the center.

3   Holding the rolled tail firmly, fold ribbon to outside at an angle.

4   Roll tail along folded edge until you roll to the fold.

5   Flare the top of the ribbon slightly as you roll.

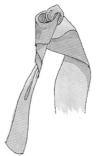

6   As you near the end of the fold, fold the ribbon to the outside again at an angle.

7   Repeat the process of rolling and folding to make all the "petals".

8   To finish, twist the end straight down and secure it with a thin wire.

Ribbon Size	Yardage	Rose Dia.
#40	2.5 yds	4 in.
#16	2. yds	4 in.
#9	1.5 yds	3 in.
#5	22 in.	2 in.
#3	18 in.	1 in.

How to Make Your Own Ribbons

What do you do when just the right ribbon can't be found? Make your own! Extra fabric can be ordered at the same time you place an order for bridal or bridemaid's dresses. Make the perfect "ribbons" from fabrics and combinations.

One Sided Ribbon

1 Cut a piece of fabric that is as long as needed but twice as wide as needed (4" for a 2" width).

2 Lay the fabric face down and fold over the edges to the center of the back. Iron them in place.

3 Cut strips of fusible web* as wide as the ribbon will be. Lay them end to end, inside the fabric. Iron the back and front to bond everything in place.

> *Fusible web is a papery material constructed with adhesive fibers. The adhesive is released when the material is heated by being ironed. It bonds together any fabrics that it is placed between. Fabric glue, hot glue and sewing can all be used instead of fusible web.

Double Sided Ribbon

1 Decide the desired length and width. Add 1/2" onto both and cut two strips of fabric to that size. (For a 2" width, cut 2 1/2" of fabric)

Lay the fabric face down and turn a 1/4" hem all the way around. Iron the hem in place

2 Cut strips of fusible web* to 1/2" and lay them under the hem. Iron the hems again, being careful not to iron the exposed fusible web.

3 Lay the ribbons back to back, lining up the edges. Iron them on either side to bond them together.

Ribbon With Edging

1 Cut two strips of fabric to the desired length and width. Cut a strip of fusible web* to fit and place it between the fabric. Make sure both "good" sides are facing out. Iron the fabric to bond it together.

2 Cut the edging to the same length as the fabric, fold it in half lengthwise and iron it down. Your edging may be bias tape or narrow ribbon.

3 Cut strips of fusible web to the same width and length as the edging. Tuck the web inside the folded edging. Lay one strip along one side of the fabric, and carefully iron it in place. Do the same for the other side and both ends of the fabric ribbon.

The Full Wrap means that an object is covered completely by overlapping the ribbon (or fabric) as it is wrapped around. Here we have a basket handle as an example.

1 The ribbon needs to be at least 2 1/2 times as long as the handle. Glue one end of the ribbon to the end of the handle.

2 Wrap the ribbon around the handle, overlapping the ribbon and covering the handle.

3 Glue the ribbon down at the other end of the handle. Make two small bows and glue them over either end of the handle.

The Loose Wrap means that a ribbon is wound around the object, but is not pulled tight. We will use another basket handle as an example.

1 Glue one end of the ribbon to one end of the handle.

2 Wrap the ribbon around the handle but only allow it to touch as it comes across the top. As the ribbon crosses the top of the handle, glue it in place before the next wrap.

3 Glue the ribbon in place at the other end of the handle. Make two small bows and glue them over the ends.

How To Wrap With Ribbons

The French Wrap is done by crossing two ribbons over an object and twisting them as they cross. It allows the object to show through. We will use a headband as an example.

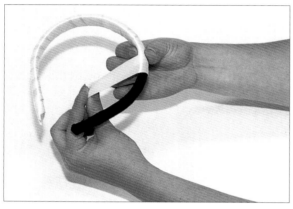

1 Wrap a head band with ribbon. Follow the instructions for the Full Wrap.

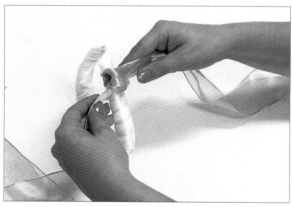

2 Measure the length of the headband and times it by 4. Cut a ribbon that size. Find the center of the ribbon and tie it in a knot over one end of the headband.

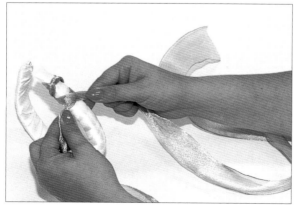

3 Wrap the ends around the back and cross them over at the top of the headband.

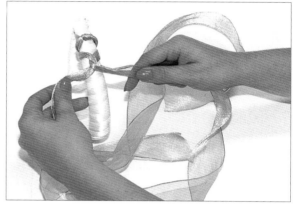

4 Where the ribbons are crossed, twist them until the ends switch across to the opposite sides.

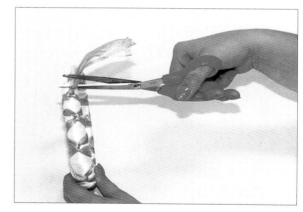

5 Continue by wrapping the ends around the back and twisting them over the top again. When you reach the other end, tie them in a knot and cut off any excess.

Renaissance Knots and Bows are made in a similar fashion to the French Wrap. We will wrap the stems of an arm bouquet as an example.

1 Wrap the stems with ribbon, using the Full Wrap method. Begin at the bottom and finish under the flowers.

2 Times the length of the stems by 6 for knots and cut a ribbon to that length. For bows, times the length by 10. Begin by finding the center of the ribbon length and tying it in a knot at the bottom of the stems.

3 For Knots: Wrap the ribbon around the back and cross it over the front. Tie a knot on the top, then wrap the ends around again.

4 For Bows: Tie a simple bow over the knot. Wrap the ends around the back and cross them over the top. Tie another simple bow on top, then wrap the ends around again to make the next bow.

5 To finish, knot the ribbon just under the flowers. Allow any excess ribbon to hang down as tails. Make a medium to large bow and wire or glue it in place just under the flowers.

Wrapping Gifts

This is where finishing a bow with ribbon instead of wire becomes really useful (See page 5).

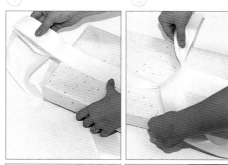

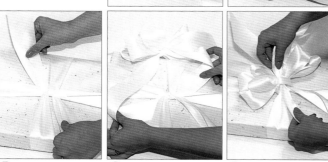

Boxes

There are many variations to this technique, but this way will work for any box.

1 Wrap a length of ribbon around one side of the box, beginning on the top.

2 Twist the ribbon around itself at the top and then wrap it around the other side of the box.

3 Cut the ribbon at the top and knot the two ends together. Make a bow and finish it with ribbon. Wrap the ties from the bow around the knot on the box and tie them together under the bow.

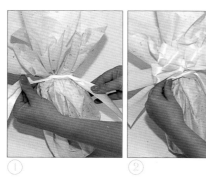

Bottles

1 Cover the bottle with paper, tissue or cellophane. Keep it in place by tying a length of ribbon around the neck.

2 Make a bow, finishing it with ribbon. Wrap the ties from the bow around the neck of the bottle, over the other ribbon. Tie the ends together in front, under the bow.

Gift Baskets

1 Place the basket (or any container) in the center of the tissue, paper or cellophane and pull the ends up to the top of the basket.

2 Tie the wrapping with a length of ribbon around the top.

3 Make a bow and finish it with ribbon. Tie the bow around the top, over the other ribbon. Knot it under the front of the bow.

You will need the following tools and supplies to make the projects in this chapter.

Tools

- Wire Cutters
- Scissors
- Glue Gun and Glue Sticks
- Yardstick
- Pruning Shears
- Serrated Knife
- Bouquet Stand

OR

- Substitute for bouquet stand

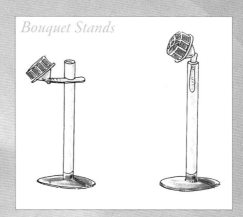

Bouquet Stands

Supplies

- 18" Floral Wire, light and medium gauges
- Floral Tape (corsage tape)
- Wooden Picks
- Floral Pins
- Corsage Pins
- Bouquet Holders

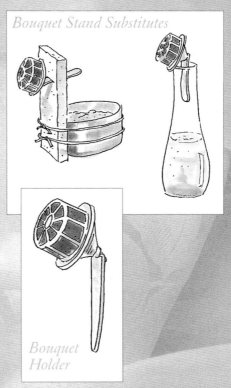

Bouquet Stand Substitutes

Bouquet Holder

Cascading Tulips

Instructions

1 Holder and Ribbon. Place the holder in the stand (See pg. 17). With 3 1/2' of ribbon, make 2", 3" and 4" loops and two 12" tails. With 7' of ribbon, make 4", 5", 7" and 9" loops with a 12" and a 20" tail. Cut the remaining ribbon in half and make two, double loops (See pg. 7–Wired Loops). Place them as shown.

2 Tulips. Cut five to 6". Place one in the center of the ribbons and the others evenly spaced around it. Cut the rest to 7", 10" and 15". Stagger them in the lower area, facing down.

3 Camellia and Ivy. Cut four, 2" and one, 6" camellia. Cut the ivy bush apart at the base, leaving the various lengths intact. Cascade the longer stems from the bottom of the holder and spread the shorter ones around the upper area.

4 Lisianthus. Cut three to 6" and one to 8". Place the 6" around the central tulip and the 8" in the bottom, with the buds cascading below it.

5 Alstromeria. Cut all to 5" and fill in the body of the bouquet.

6 Stephanotis. Cut a 10", 8" and eight 5" stems. Place the longer ones in the lower area and use the rest to fill in around the ribbons.

7 Pearls. Use wire or wood picks to extend the stems of the pearls. Make one 10" and the rest 6". Cascade the 10" from the bottom and use the rest to fill in.

Materials

- 1 Bouquet holder and stand
- 4 Yards (white) sheer ribbon, size 9
- 8 Stems (peach) tulips
- 1 Spray (green) camellia leaves (3 stems)
- 1 Bush (green) ivy (10 stems)
- 1 Spray (white) lisianthus (4 blooms)
- 1 Spray (white) alstromeria (5 blooms)
- 2 Sprays (white) stephanotis (10 blooms)
- 8 Sprays (white) 4" pearl loops

French Twist Headband

Instructions

1. Headband and Ribbon. Glue one end of the white ribbon to one end of the headband. Wrap the ribbon around, overlapping it to cover the headband completely. (See full wrap pg. 13).

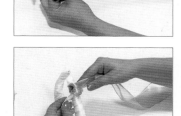

2. Glue the center of the gold ribbon to the inside of the headband at one end. Knot it on the top side and wrap it around the back. As the ribbons come back over the top, cross them. Then twist them so they head off in opposite directions again. (See French wrap pg. 14).

3. Knot the ribbons together at the other end, cut them and glue the ends to the inside of the headband.

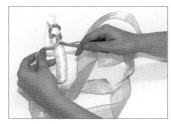

Materials

- 1 (Padded) headband
- 3 1/2 Yards (white) satin ribbon, size 9
- 5 1/2 Yards (gold) metallic ribbon, size 9

Kiss In The Clouds

Instructions

1 Barrette and Veil. Use a light gauge floral wire to attach the loops on the top of the veil to the barrette. Once it is fastened securely, use hot glue to scrunch it down, covering the barrette with the veil.

2 Ribbon. Make 6 separate bows with six, 3" loops each. Cut the wires under the bows to 1/2" and glue them in place over the veil as shown.

Materials

- 1 (French clip) hair barrette
- 1 (White) fingertip length veil
- 3 Yards (white) sheer ribbon, size 9

Instructions

1 Place the bouquet holder in the stand. (See pg. 17).

2 Roses. Cut all to 6". Place the largest blooms in first and spread them apart evenly. Add the smaller blooms last to fill in.

3 Ribbon. Cut twelve, 12" strips. Make a two loop bow with tails from each strip. Place the bows between the roses to fill in empty areas and add texture to the bouquet.

4 Ivy. Remove the leaves from the stems and glue them to the back of the holder, facing out. You will form a ring around the back to cover the flower stems.

Materials

- 1 (Foam) bouquet holder and stand
- 10 Blooms (white and pastel) assorted medium roses
- 25 Blooms (white and pastel) assorted small roses
- 4 Yards (white) sheer ribbon, size 9
- 2 Stems (green) ivy

Instructions

1. **Headband, Comb and Veil.**
   Glue the veil to the underside of the headband. Attach a comb using a needle and thread to the underside of the veil.

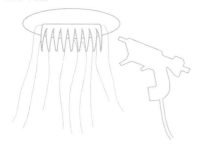

2. **Ribbon.** Cover the top of the headband by gluing a strip of ribbon over it. Make a 10-loop floral bow. The loops on both sides should measure 5 1/2", 4 1/2", 4", 3 1/2" and 3". Make a single 2" last loop and thread the wire through it when wiring the bow. Trim off any tails or excess and glue the bow to the top of the headband.

Materials ❧

- 1 (White) crescent headband
- 1 (Clear) hair comb
- 1 (White) fingertip length veil
- 3 Yards (white) striped satin ribbon, size 40

Garden Wedding

Instructions

1. Hollyhocks, Campanula and Foxglove. Lay the tall flowers in a narrow fan pattern as shown. Stagger the heights to keep them spread out.

2. Hydrangeas and Alstromeria. Lay the smaller hydrangea in-between the tall flowers to fill in. Stagger the larger hydrangea and the alstromeria in the lower area of the bouquet.

3. Wire all the stems together and trim them 12" under the lowest flowers. Tape over the stems with floral tape.

4. Ribbon. Cut 30" of white ribbon and do a full wrap over the stems (See pg. 13). Cut 72" of cream ribbon and do renaissance knots over the stems (See pg. 15). Use the rest of the ribbon to make a multiple-ribbon bow. Loop the ribbons six times on each side, making 5" loops. The tails should be about 20" long (See pg. 9). Wire or glue the bow just under the flowers.

Materials

- 2 Stems (cream) hollyhocks
- 6 Stems (lavender) campanula
- 1 Stem (peach) foxglove
- 3 Sprays (white) snowball hydrangea (9 blooms)
- 3 Stems (pink) hydrangea
- 1 Stem (white) alstromeria
- 7 Yards (white) satin ribbon, size 9
- 8 Yards (cream) wired satin ribbon, size 9

Pearls and Picot

Materials

- 1 (White) pearl band
- 7 1/2 Yards (white) picot ribbon, size 1
- 4 (White) satin flowers with pearl centers

Instructions

1 Pearl band. Wire the ends of the band together and tape over them with white floral tape.

2 Ribbon. Cut a 22" strip and glue one end of it to the back of the band. Wrap the ribbon around the band, allowing the pearls to show through underneath. Glue down the other end. Make a bow with twenty, 2" loops. Cut the remaining ribbon into 4 long strips and glue them to the back of the bow. Glue the bow and tails to the back of the band.

3 Flowers. Cut the wire stems off the flowers and glue them in a tight cluster in the center of the bow.

Simple Elegance

Materials

- 1 Stem (blush) large rose
- 3 Stems (pink) medium roses
- 3 Stems (white) medium roses
- 2 Sprays (pink) lisianthus (6 blooms)
- 2 Sprays (white) bouvardia (4 blooms)
- 3 Sprays (white) lilac (6 blooms)
- 2 Sprays (peach) lilac (4 blooms)
- 10 Stems (green) preserved plumosa fern
- 2 Feet (white) satin ribbon, size 9
- 2 Yards (white/pink) striped ribbon, size 9
- 2 Yards (white) picot ribbon, size 1

Instructions

1 Flowers and Fern. Place all the fern in one hand and arrange it to form the general shape of the bouquet. Insert the flowers one at a time in the order listed. As each flower is added, keep the similar types apart so the bouquet doesn't get clumpy. Adjust the flowers so the blooms are all at about the same height.

Trim the stems 9" below the flowers and wire them all together. Wrap the stems with floral tape.

2 Ribbons. Do a full wrap on the stems with the size 9, white ribbon (See pg. 13). Make a floral bow with the white/pink ribbon. It should have two 2", four 3" and two 4" loops (See pg. 8). The rest of the ribbon should be cut in half and used as tails. Wire or glue the bow to the top of the stems. Cut the picot ribbon into four equal sections. Stagger the lengths and wrap them around the bouquet, knotting them together in the center of the bow.

Loose and Casual Bow Barrette
Instructions

1 Ribbon and Barrette. Glue strips of ribbon over the top of the barrette to cover it.

Make a bow using both ribbons (See "multiple ribbon bows"). The ribbons should be looped 5 times on each side, keeping the loops between 2" and 3". Cut the rest of the pink ribbon into 2 strips and glue them to the back of the bow as tails. Cut the mauve ribbon into 3 strips and also glue them to the back, staggering the lengths.

2 Rose. Glue the bow with tails to the top of the barrette. Glue the ribbon rose (or any decoration) to the center of the bow.

Materials
- 2 1/2 yards (pink) satin ribbon, 1/4"
- 2 1/2 yards (mauve) satin ribbon, 1/8"
- 1 (French clip) hair barrette
- 1 (Mauve) ribbon rose with leaves

Bridesmaid's Headpiece
Instructions

1 Ribbon. Make a 7 inch wide, 8 loop Loopy bow with 8 inch tails (See page 8). Set aside.

2 Comb and pearl loops. Wrap the stems of the pearl loops around the teeth of the comb. Position one on either end and two in the middle leaning forward and backwards.

3 Bow. Hot glue the bow to the comb and arrange the pearl loops in-between the bow loops.

Materials
- 2 yards (off white) wired ribbon
- 3 inch comb
- 4 pearl loops

Materials

- 1 (white) 4" round basket
- 3 Yards (celedon) moiré ribbon, size 9
- 10 Ounces (assorted) dried flower petals

Fanciful Flower Girl Instructions

1. Basket and Ribbon. Cut 25" of ribbon and wrap the basket handle. (See pg. 13) Cut two 10" sections and divide the rest of the ribbon in half. Make two floral bows (See pg. 8). Each will have two 2" and two 1 1/2" loops with two 5" tails. Use the 10" strips to finish the bows (See pg. 5). Tie or glue them on to the bottom of the handles.

2. Petals. Fill the basket with dried, fresh or silk petals for the flower girl to toss. The basket can also be used to hold a small arrangement.

Materials

- 1 (white) 5" battenburgh pillow
- 4 1/2 Yards (white) satin ribbon, 1/16" width

Battenburgh Ring Pillow Instructions

Cut a 44" piece of ribbon and thread it through an upholstery needle. Push the needle through the center of the pillow and pull half the ribbon through. Knot the ribbon together so it is securely in place and attached to the pillow.

With the rest of the ribbon, make a loopy bow with twelve 2" loops and ten tails of various lengths. Once the bow is wired together, cut off excess wire and lay the bow in the center of the pillow.

To attach the bow to the pillow, tie the long, threaded tails around the center of the bow. Tie the rings in place.

Necklace Corsage Instructions

1. Orchids. Cut the stems to 1/2" and tape them together with floral tape.

2. Cosmos. Cut all to 3" and tape them to the sides of the orchids. Glue or tape the leaves around the back of the flowers.

3. Cording. Make 3, 1" loops. Wire each loop at the base. Tape them in place

Materials

- 2 Blooms (white) orchids
- 3 Blooms (yellow) cosmos
- 1/2 Yard (gold) cording
- 1 1/2 Yards (teal) satin ribbon, size 9

Wrist Corsage Instructions

1. Rose and Orchid. Cut the rose and orchid stems to 1" and tape them together with floral tape.

2. Berries. Cut all to 4" and make two clusters, staggering the heights. Tape the clusters around the other flowers.

3. Ribbon. Make a bow with three 1 1/2" loops using the sheer ribbon. Wire the bow to the bottom of the flowers and tape over it. Lay the flowers over the center of the other ribbon and wire them together. Use the ribbon to tie the corsage onto the wrist or neck.

Materials

- 1 Bloom (white) rose
- 1 Bloom (green) orchid
- 6 Blooms (cream) bridal berries
- 1/2 Yard (gold) sheer ribbon, size 9
- 1 1/2 Yard (gold/black) ribbon, size 9

Shoulder Corsage Instructions

1. Orchids. Cut the stem to 14" and bend it over a shoulder to find the natural balance point. It will hang longer in the front than in the back.

2. Gardenia. Cut the stems to 2" and glue each flower in place. Glue larger flowers near the top of the shoulder.

3. Ribbon. Make 4 loopy bows. Make two with fourteen, 2" loops, one with eight, 1 1/2" loops and one with six, 1" loops. Glue the bows between the gardenias. Glue three, 7" strips of ribbon to hang down the back, under the bow.

Materials

- 1 Stem (lavender) mini orchids (8-10 blooms)
- 4 Blooms (white) gardenia
- 3 Yards (burgundy) picot ribbon, size 1

Decorating the Ceremony

You will need the following tools and supplies to make the projects in this chapter.

Tools

- Wire Cutters
- Scissors
- Glue Gun/Glue Sticks
- Yardstick
- Measuring Tape
- Pruning Shears
- Serrated Knife

Supplies

- 18" Floral Wire, light, medium and heavy gauges
- Spool Wire, medium gauge
- Floral Tape
- Pew Clips

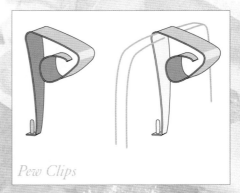

Pew Clips

Cloudy Bows
Instructions

1 Lay the sheer ribbon over the tulle and make a multiple-ribbon bow (See pg. 9). The bow should have eight, 4" loops and 20" tails. Add the remaining tulle as extra bow tails.

2 Finish the bow with heavy gauge wire if the wire will be bent over the pew as the hanger. Wrap the wire with floral tape so it doesn't scratch the pew.

Finish the bow with a light wire if it will be hung with a pew clip. To attach the bow either glue it on or wrap the wire around the clip.

Materials ✻

(for each)
❧ 3 1/2 Yards (opaque) sheer ribbon, size 40
❧ 4 1/2 Yards (white) tulle, 6" width

Cloudy Garland
Instructions

1 Measure the length between the pew bows. The bows may be set on every pew or every other pew depending on your preference. Times the length by 2.5 to determine how much sheer ribbon you will need between each bow. Times the length by 6 to determine the tulle. Cut the tulle into 3 equal sections.

2 The garland sections are made by wiring the ends of the tulle and wrapping around them loosely with the sheer ribbon.

3 The garland can be connected to the bow by gluing or wiring it to the pew clip or to the bow wire.

Materials ✻

❧ (Opaque) sheer ribbon, size 40
❧ (White) tulle, 6" width
The materials you use should match bows

Aisle Decorations

Green Garland
Instructions

1. Measuring. You will need to measure the length between the bows and multiply it by 2.5. Multiply that total by the number of bows to calculate the total length of the garland. (Don't forget you need one for each side of the aisle).

2. Making. Lay a few pieces of fern with the tips pointing away and the stems pointing towards you. Wrap them together with spool wire. Lay a few more pieces over them, in the same direction. Allow the tips of the second bunch to cover the stems of the first. Wrap the spool wire around both to connect them. Continue laying a few pieces at a time and wiring them to the others until the garland is as long as needed.

Flower Clusters
Instructions

1. Lilies. Stagger the lilies and wrap the stems together with wire. Cut the stems off 7" below the lower bloom.

2. To Hang. Bend the stem of the lilies into a hook shape. Adjust the blooms so they are facing out and hang them over the center of the bow.

Materials ✻ ❧ (Fresh) plumosa fern

Materials ✻

(for each)
❧ 2 Blooms (pink) lilies

Aisle Candles

Instructions

1 Fern. Place the ends of the fern just below the candle tray. Wrap a floral wire around them and the candle stand to keep them in place.

2 Ribbon and Tulle. Lay the sheer ribbon over the tulle and make a multiple-ribbon bow (See pg. 9). The bow should have eight, 4" loops and 20" tails. Add the remaining tulle as extra bow tails. Wrap the bow wire around the ends of the fern, where they are wired to the candle stand. Wind the fern and bow tails around the candle stand.

Materials

- 3-5 Stems (green) fresh plumosa fern
- 3 1/2 Yards (opaque) sheer ribbon, size 40
- 4 1/2 Yards (white) tulle, 6" width

Instructions

1 Ribbon and Tulle. Make three cloudy bows (See pg. 30). Twist the wires from the bows together to make a giant bow.

2 Leaves and Lily. Cut the leaves into 6" sections. Wrap a floral wire on each section to give it a bendable "stem". (The same can be done to the lily if it is fresh.)

Tuck the lily in the center of the bow and the leaves all around it. Keep them in place by wrapping the wire "stems" around the bow wire.

Once in place, wrap all with floral tape. Bend the wire into a hook shape and hang it on the candelabra or use separate wires to wire it in place.

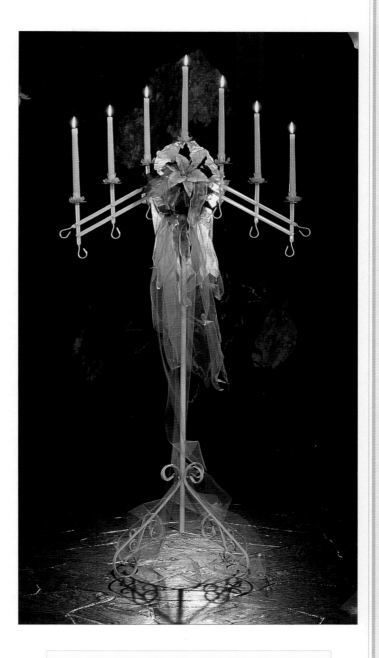

Materials

(for each)
- 10 1/2 Yards (opaque) sheer ribbon, size 40
- 13 1/2 Yards (white) tulle, 6" width
- 2 Stems (green) fresh salal leaves
- 1 Bloom (pink) latex lily

Garden Gazebo

Instructions

The exact measurements will vary for every gazebo. Measure the height and width before you buy the tulle. The one pictured is 9' tall and 6' wide.

1 Tulle. Cut two 10' and one 8' lengths. Wrap both ends of the 8' piece with wire. Wire one end of each 10' piece. First hang the long pieces on the sides by wrapping the wire onto the gazebo. Hang the shorter piece across the top, just above the side pieces.

2 Ribbons. Make a layered bow (See pg. 9). Use the satin ribbon for the bottom bow making ten, 7" loops and two 30" tails. Use the striped sheer ribbon on top. It should have ten, 5" loops and two 20" tails. Once they are wired together, wrap the wires with floral tape and bend them into a hook shape. Make another for the other side.

3 Cut a 4 yard length of striped sheer ribbon and wrap it around the tulle across the top of the gazebo. Wire the ends to keep it in place. Divide the rest of the ribbon in half and add them as extra tails to each bow. Hang the bows on either side to cover the wires that hold the tulle in place.

4 Fern and Roses. Wrap a wire around the bottom of each fern stem. Add 8 stems behind each bow. Tuck it in place and wrap the wire onto the bow or the gazebo. Remove the petals from the roses and sprinkle them at the last minute inside the gazebo.

Materials

- 10 Yards (ivory) tulle, 60" width
- 15 Yards (ivory striped) sheer ribbon, 3" width
- 12 Yards (ivory) wired satin ribbon, size 40
- 16 Stems (green) fresh sprengerii fern
- 12 Blooms (white) fresh roses

To make the wreath, see page 42

Instructions

1 Salal. Cut the stems into 5" sections. Face 2 sections in one direction and 3 in the opposite. Wire them together in the center where the stems cross.

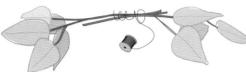

Once the clusters are made, wire them all around the arch in an alternating pattern.

2 Tulle. Begin on the bottom of one side. Weave the tulle in and out of the arch. Keep the weave loose and full using all the tulle.

3 Pearls. Begin by wiring the center of the pearl stand to the top of the arch. Drape the ends down either side, wiring them in place as you go.

4 Ribbon. Make a floral bow (See pg. 8). Make two 3", six 6" and six 8" loops. Set it aside. Wire the center of the remaining ribbon to the top of the arch. Loop it down the sides, keeping it in place with wires as you go. Wire the bow to the arch last. Place it just to the right of the center or directly in the center, depending on your preference.

5 Lilies. Cut the stems to 4" and wire them onto the arch in an alternating pattern.

Materials

- 20 Stems (green) fresh salal
- 50 Yards (white) tulle, 6" width
- 15 Yards (white) pearls, 1/4" width
- 20 Yards (white) wired satin ribbon, size 40
- 8 Blooms (pink) latex lilies

Decorating the Reception

You will need the following tools and supplies to make the projects in this chapter.

Tools

- Wire Cutters
- Scissors
- Glue Gun/Glue Sticks
- Yardstick
- Pruning Shears
- Serrated Knife

Supplies

- 18" Floral Wire, light, medium and heavy gauges
- Spool Wire, medium gauge
- Corsage Pins
- Floral Tape
- Wooden Picks
- Water Tubes

Ribbons and Bows
Instructions

1. Salal and Plumosa. Lay the salal, piece by piece down the front of the table. Begin in the center and face the tips out in either direction. Lay the plumosa over it in the same manner. Allow the plumosa to drape off the front of the table.

2. Ribbon. Cut the length in half and set one aside. Cut the other half into seven, 2' sections. With each section make a loopy bow with eight, 4" loops and two tails. (See pg. 8)

3. Tulle. Lay the remaining length of lace ribbon over the tulle. Begin on one end and drape it loosely across the front of the table weaving it in and out of the greens. Place one bow in the center of the table and three, spaced evenly on either side.

Materials

For a 20' table
- 25 Stems (green) fresh salal
- 50 Stems (green) fresh plumosa
- 30 Yards (white) lace ribbon, size 16
- 15 Yards (white) tulle, 6" width

Adding Flowers
Instructions

1. Roses. Stagger two roses together and cut the stems 4" below the blooms. Wire them together. Make six more.

2. Ivy. The lengths shown vary from 4" to 6" but any lengths will work. Add 4 stems of green and 2 stems of variegated ivy to each rose cluster. Wire them to the stems then tape the whole thing with floral tape.

3. Place one rose cluster in the center of each bow. Bend the wire stem over the top of the bow and pin it to the tablecloth if necessary. Adjust the roses as desired.

Materials

- 14 Blooms (pink) silk roses
- 28 Stems (green) silk ivy
- 14 Stems (variegated) ivy

Candlelight Dinner Table

Top view of table

Materials

For an 8' table
- 5 (Clear) 4" bubble bowls
- 5 (White) votive candles
- 10 Stems (green) fresh sprengerii
- 3 Yards (pink/white) tapestry ribbon, 3" width
- 12 Blooms (white) fresh roses

Instructions

1 Bowls and Candles. Spread the bowls down the center of the table. Place a candle in each.

2 Sprengerii. Lay the fern end to end down the center of the table. Cover the stem of one with the tip of the next and snake it gently back and forth around the candles.

3 Ribbon and Roses. Weave the ribbon back and forth, following the fern. Tuck it and loop it slightly to give it body. Lay the rose blooms on top of the ribbon, alternating them all down the table. (A small water tube is needed for each rose if the set up is done more than an hour before the dinner.)

Floating Centerpiece

Instructions

1. Bowl and Gardenia. Place the bowl in the center of the table with the gardenia floating in it.

2. Sprengerii and Pearls. Lay the fern end to end around the bowl, overlapping them slightly. Drape the pearls back and forth over the fern.

3. Ribbon. Cut a 2-yard length and weave it around the fern and pearls. Cut the rest into 5 equal sections and make 5 loopy bows (See pg. 8). Each bow will have six, 2" loops and four tails of various lengths. Space the bows evenly around the bowl and spread the tails out onto the table.

4. Roses. Cut all to 6" and lay one at each place (Table seats 10). Remove the petals from the two left over and sprinkle them around the ribbon tails.

Materials

- 1 (Clear) 8" bubble bowl
- 1 (Fresh) gardenia (sub: rose, camellia or peony)
- 5 Stems (green) fresh sprengerii
- 1 Yard (white) pearls, 1/4" width
- 12 Yards (ivory) picot ribbon, size 1
- 12 Stems (white) fresh roses

Traditional Topiary

Instructions

1 Topiary, Pot and Moss. Place the plant in the pot and cover the top with moss.

2 Ribbon. Make three loopy bows (See pg. 8). Each will have ten, 3" loops and two 6" tails. Wire two bows clustered together on one side of the topiary ball. Place the other in the pot on the opposite side. Wrap the remaining ribbon around the trunk connecting the upper and lower bows.

Materials

- 1 (Fresh ivy) ball topiary
- 1 (Terra-cotta) 6" clay pot
- Sphagnum Moss
- 8 Yards (peach sherbet) silk ribbon, size 9

Napkin Bows

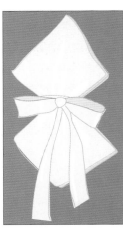

You will need an additional 24" of the same ribbon for each napkin bow.

1 Fold the napkins in a square. Gather the sides in and tie the length of ribbon around the center. Tie a simple, shoelace-style bow.

Wedding Ring

Instructions

1 Wreath and Ribbon. Glue one end of the ribbon to the back of the wreath. Wrap it around, covering the wreath with a full wrap. (See pg. 13)

2 Tulle. Cut 1 yard off and set it aside. Wrap the rest around the wreath over the ribbon. Cut the yard strip into single 12"x12" squares and wire each one as a single loop.

3 Ivy. Lay the stems all around the wreath, weaving them back and forth in a random pattern. Keep them in place by pushing a floral pin over the stems every so often.

4 Roses. Cut all to 4". Add the large roses first. Make 5 or 6 small clusters around the wreath. They can be glued in place or inserted directly into the wreath. To push it in, you will need to make a small hole in the tulle with a knife where the rose will be placed. Add the smaller roses around the larger ones, spreading out the colors and filling in empty areas.

5 Tulle. Glue in the tulle loops to cover up stems and fill in the empty areas.

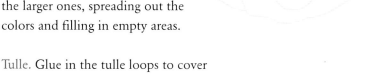

Materials

- 1 (Straw) 36" round wreath
- 10 Yards (ivory) acetate ribbon, size 40
- 8 Yards (ivory) tulle, 36" width
- 18 Stems (green) medium ivy
- 12 Stems (green) small ivy
- 24 Blooms (assorted pinks) large roses
- 40 Blooms (assorted pastels) wild roses

Instructions

1. Ribbon. Make a loopy bow with sixteen, 4" loops and four, 4" tails (See pg. 8). Cut the remaining ribbon into six unequal strips.

2. Pearls. Cut six, 8" strips and glue the ends into the bow as pearl loops. Cut the rest into four unequal sections. Make two sets of extra tails by gathering three strips of ribbon and two strips of pearls and wiring them together in the center.

3. Cage. Glue or wire the tails to the top of the cage. Glue or wire the bow over them.

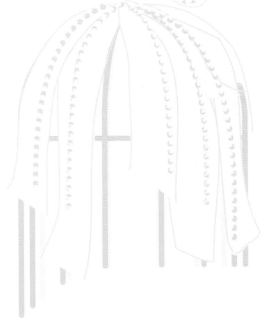

Materials

- 11 Yards (white) sheer ribbon, size 9
- 7 Yards (white) pearls, 1/16"
- 1 (Green) wire birdcage

Cake Toppers

Instructions

1 French Ribbon. Divide the ribbon in half and make two loopy bows with twelve 5" loops and three sets of tails in various lengths (See pg. 8).

2 Savoy Ribbon. Make one loopy bow with four 5" loops and three sets of tails.

3 Sheer Ribbon. Cut 3 1/2 yards and make a loopy bow with sixteen, 4" loops and four sets of tails. Lay it on top of a French ribbon bow and wire them together. Place this bow on the top of the cake.

Divide the remaining sheer ribbon in half and make two loopy bows with twelve, 3" loops and three sets of tails.

Lay one over the Savoy bow and the other over the remaining French ribbon bow.

Place the French and sheer bow on the third layer and the Savoy and sheer bow on the bottom layer. Adjust the tails of all and trim them as desired.

4 Orchids. Remove the flowers from the stems and make a simple cluster on the second layer. Lay the rest in and around the bows as desired.

Materials

- 10 Yards (white) French ribbon, size 9
- 4 Yards (white) savoy ribbon, size 40
- 13 Yards (white) sheer ribbon, size 9
- 8 Stems (white) fresh dendrobium orchids

Cake Table and Bows

Instructions

1 Tulle. Drape the tulle all around the cake table. Allow it to spill over the edge for 12" to 18".

2 Ribbon and Orchids. Gather the tulle in several spots around the table. At each spot, wrap 1 yard of ribbon around the gather. Pin the ribbon and tulle to the tablecloth. Lay the two stems of orchids in the center of the ribbon and tie a simple bow over them. If the weight of the flowers is too much, use more straight pins into the tablecloth to support it.

Materials

(for each)
- 6 Yards (white) tulle, 60" width
- 1 Yard (white) savoy ribbon, size 40
- 2 Stems (white) fresh dendrobium orchids

Cake Knife and Server

Instructions

1 Orchids and Plumosa. Remove the flowers from the stems and insert a 6" floral wire into each. Tape over the flower and wire with floral tape to hold them together. Add a fern tip behind each flower and tape it in place.

2 Ribbon. Cut the ribbon in half. Tie the lengths onto the cake knife and server. Lay a few orchids over the ribbon. Tie a simple bow to keep the orchids in place.

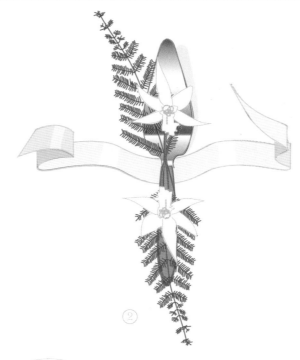

Materials

- 2 Stems (white) dendrobium orchids
- 1 Stem (green) plumosa
- 1 Yard (white) savoy ribbon, size 9

Wrapped Favor

Materials ✖

(for each)
- 20" (White) tulle, 6" width
- 1 Chocolate truffle
- 12" (White) French ribbon, size 9

This is the basic method for wrapping any type of favor.

- *The tulle can be substituted with pretty paper, fabric, cellophane, Mylar or very wide ribbon.*

- *The truffle can be substituted with almonds, potpourri, candy, bath salts or trinkets.*

- *The ribbon can be wide or thin and of any type. Some stores are even able to print the bride and groom's names along with the date on the tails of the bow.*

Instructions

1 Tulle. Cut the tulle in half and cross them over each other in opposite directions.

2 Truffle and Ribbon. Place the truffle in the center and gather the tulle up around it. Tie it off with the ribbon, making a simple bow in the front.

Potted Favor

Instructions

1 Pot and Plant. Put the plant in the pot. Cover the top with a touch of moss.

2 Ribbon. Glue the center of the ribbon to the back of the pot. Wrap it around the front and tie a simple bow.

Materials

- 1 (Terra-cotta) 2" clay pot
- 1 (Variegated) 2" fresh ivy plant
- 18" (Ivory) wired satin ribbon, size 9

- *The pot can be painted to match any color scheme. Small baskets or other mini containers are also easily substituted.*

- *The plant can be any green or blooming fresh plant. It may also be silk or dried. It looks darling to have a potted favor at every place with a larger version as the table centerpiece.*

- *The ribbon, of course, can be of any size, style or color depending on the wedding theme.*

Sheer Bow

You will need 2 yards of sheer (white) ribbon, size 9. Cut the length in half and make two loopy bows. Each will have four, 1" loops and two 1" tails. Finish each with a length of ribbon and tie them onto the bottom of the glasses. (See pg. 5, 8)

Simple Layered Bows

You will need 1 yard of wired (gold) ribbon, size 9 and 1 yard of (opaque) sheer ribbon, size 40. Cut the lengths in half and lay the gold over the sheer ribbon. Wrap each around a toasting glass and tie a simple shoelace-type bow.

Delicate Picot Bow

You will need 5 yards of (white) picot ribbon, size 1. Cut the ribbon in half and make two loopy bows. Each will have twelve, 2" loops and two, 10" tails. Use the remaining ribbon to tie off the bows (See pg. 5, 8). Glue three small (lavender) ribbon roses in a cluster to the center of each bow. Tie the bows to the base of the toasting glasses.